OVERHEAD WRITING LESSONS

STRONG SENTENCES

by Carol Rawlings Miller
and Sarah Glasscock

NEW YORK • TORONTO • LONDON • AUCKLAND • SYDNEY
MEXICO CITY • NEW DELHI • HONG KONG • BUENOS AIRES

Teaching *Resources*

This book is dedicated to Jack.
—CRM

Acknowledgments
Sincerest thanks are due to Jeanne and
Milton Miller and Charles and Joan Rawlings,
for being devoted, babysitting grandparents,
and to my husband James Miller, for patience.

More than one editor made this series possible.
I really am indebted to Ellen Ungaro—not only
for her expertise and encouragement, but
for her sense of humor. I also wish to thank
Virginia Dooley; she has been, amongst other
things, patient. And to Wendy Murray, for
weighing in helpfully, many thanks.
—CRM

Cover Design by Josué Castilleja
Cover Illustration by Eric Brace
Interior Design by Brian LaRossa

Book ISBN 0-439-56818-8
Product ISBN 0-439-22259-1
Copyright © 2005 by Carol Rawlings Miller and Sarah Glasscock
All rights reserved.
Printed in the U.S.A.

1 2 3 4 5 6 7 8 9 10   40   12 11 10 09 08 07 06 05

Contents

Introduction

How does one write a strong sentence? Such a simple activity should be easy to explain, but it is often difficult to make generalizations about good writing. Authors have different writing styles, from the spare language of Ernest Hemingway to the more intricate sentences of Charles Dickens. The sentences in the breathless climax of an Edgar Allan Poe story contrast sharply with the measured and informative sentences of an article on the sleeping habits of bats.

Although great writing defies easy definition, we teachers still need to use generalizations to teach our students to become better writers. In looking at the examples and ranges of many authors, key elements emerge.

- **Clear and vivid language** conveys meaning and engages our minds (and sometimes, our hearts).
- **Grammatical soundness** avoids sentence logic that is confusing and permits readers to understand meaning.
- **Conventional consistency** allows readers to read text without being distracted by inexplicable changes in form.
- **Variety in sentence structure and length** keeps readers interested and involved.

▲ The Approach of This Book

Knowledge of grammar is essential in writing logical sentences and in recognizing confusing sentences. This book presents the grammatical tools to help your students write with more confidence and to edit their work more effectively. The ten lessons introduce strong sentences; focus on seven of the eight parts of speech: nouns, pronouns, adjectives, verbs, adverbs, prepositions, and conjunctions; and explore participles, subject-verb agreement, and sentence fragments and run-ons.

Even as students tackle more complex grammar skills, you may find it necessary to review more basic skills—such as the rules of capitalization and the difference between singular and plural. Students often have surprising gaps in their knowledge due to developmental quirks, curricular glitches, and the wonderful but imperfect art of teaching.

▲ Using This Book

Lessons in this book range from fundamental work on nouns to the more challenging topics of modifiers and sentence structure. You can move methodically through the book or use different lessons and activities to supplement other instructional materials.

Each lesson is accompanied by an overhead transparency and one or more reproducibles. The transparencies include quotes from well-known children's and adult authors that highlight the lesson topic, a definition of the topic and helpful information, and exercises for you and the class to work on together. The reproducibles give students more practice with each topic. We suggest that you display the overhead for reference as students work on the reproducibles.

The teaching pages display the pertinent National Language Arts Standards for each lesson. You'll also find information here about how to present the overhead transparencies and the reproducibles. Writing Connections and Reading Connections feature activities that allow students to apply the skills in their own writing and independent reading. Some lessons include a teaching tips section called Keep in Mind.

To reinforce the lessons in this book, highlight the skills you've covered when you comment on your students' writing. For example, after teaching the lesson on sentence fragments, Carol focuses on fragments in her remarks and presses students to revise their work even more than she normally would.

▲ On Teaching Standard English

Carol addresses the fact that she is teaching standard English head-on because some students resist the formality of the language. She usually explains to students that standard English is expected in academic environments and in most working situations. A poor command of standard English could have an impact on their success in the future. Students should not restrict themselves by only speaking and writing idiomatic English.

On the other hand, Carol also points out that in certain contexts idiomatic or non-standard English can be effective, powerful, and natural to use. Acknowledging the very real significance of idiomatic language can help dilute the resistance to learning and using standard English—and using it well.

▲ On Overhead Writing Lessons

Strong Sentences, *Powerful Paragraphs*, and *Exceptional Essays* comprise the Overhead Writing Lessons series of books. Each book targets and teaches specific grammar and writing skills that will make your students better and more confident writers.

Strong Sentences

National Language
Arts Standards:

▲ Uses a variety of
sentence structures

▲ Uses conventions of
capitalization in
written compositions

▲ Uses conventions of
punctuation in written
compositions

**Overhead
Transparency**

◆ Strong Sentences

Reproducible

◆ Pick the Stronger
Sentence

◆ Purpose ◆

To explain that sentences are made up of different parts of speech and to explore the idea of sentence logic

In order for students to be able to express themselves clearly and effectively, they must first understand what a complete sentence is. Then they can begin to recognize the different parts of speech and appreciate how each one can contribute to a strong sentence.

▲ Launching Activity: Strong Sentences (Overhead 1)

To give students a taste of the wide range of sentences that are possible, read aloud the quotes at the top of the overhead. Then elicit students' responses to the quotes by posing questions such as the following: *Which sentences make you want to read the rest of the book? What similarities do the sentences share? How are they different? How does each set of sentences make you feel? What do you want to know about each book?*

As you go over the definition and other information about sentences, use the quotes as examples by pointing out the nouns, pronouns, and verbs in each sentence. Before going over the exercises at the bottom of the overhead, you may want to review declarative, interrogative, exclamatory, and imperative sentences. Be sure students understand that 3 is a complete imperative sentence because the subject *you* is understood. Answers: complete: 2, 3, 6; incomplete: 1, 4, 5.

▲ Student Reproducible

After students complete the Pick the Stronger Sentence reproducible, go over it as a class. As you discuss each pair of sentences, ask students to articulate the problems with the weaker, less logical sentences. You may want to model your response to the first pair of sentences: *In the first pair, sentence A doesn't tell me anything specific. I know someone had a habit of making something, but I don't know who or what. The writer uses pronouns instead of nouns, but it's impossible to know which nouns these pronouns are replacing. Sentence B is stronger because it's very clear and specific.*

▲ Keep in Mind

Most students intuitively know a great deal about language coherence because they use language every day in many situations. As you teach the importance of sentences, remind students to *listen* to the language flowing all around them and to see where their instincts take them when they write.

Pick the Stronger Sentence
Remember that a strong sentence is complete, clear, and interesting.

Read each pair of sentences. Circle the sentence that you think is stronger.

1. A. It was not her habit to make it.
 B. It was not Della's habit to make candy for Halloween.

2. A. Della's secret pleasure was buying chocolate candy for Halloween.
 B. Buying chocolate candy was Della's secret.

3. A. On Halloween, Della surprised her sons Lon and Don by making green eggs and ham for breakfast.
 B. She surprised her sons Lon and Don by making breakfast.

4. A. Even if his mom thought it made him look like a ghost, Lon was tired of it.
 B. Lon was tired of dressing up in an old sheet, but his mother thought it made him look like a ghost.

5. A. Ringing the doorbell, Lon hoped that Mr. Hollow hadn't bought peppermint candy for Halloween—again.
 B. Lon rang the doorbell and waited for Mr. Hollow to open the door.

Now write your own strong sentence about Halloween.

_____

_____

Rewrite your sentence to make it even stronger.

_____

_____

Nouns

National Language Arts Standards:

▲ Uses nouns in written compositions

▲ Uses the conventions of capitalization

Overhead Transparency

◆ Nouns

Reproducibles

◆ Wanted by Sentences: Nouns

◆ Let's Get Specific

◆ Purpose ◆

To identify nouns and to use them with more precision

If students can't identify nouns, they'll have a hard time learning other parts of speech and locating the subject of a sentence. Many language skills such as creating subject-verb agreement are based on recognizing nouns. (Note: For a lesson on subject-verb agreement, see pages 39–40.)

Students who have no problems recognizing nouns can run into trouble, too. They are often prone to using overly general nouns repeatedly, which can make their writing dull and redundant.

▲ Launching Activity: Nouns (Overhead 2)

Call on volunteers to read the quotes on the overhead. Discuss students' reactions to the sentences. You may want to get the ball rolling by modeling your own reaction: *I love the way Jean Craighead George uses the nouns* flash *and* thunder *to describe the animals' movement. These nouns really give me a picture of the action: I can see and hear what she's writing about.* As you close the activity later, have students identify the nouns (and what they name) in each of the quotes.

After going over the bulleted information about nouns, brainstorm synonyms for the nouns in the exercises at the bottom of the overhead. Take the opportunity here to reinforce the concepts of capitalization of proper nouns and singular and plural noun forms.

▲ Student Reproducibles

Wanted by Sentences: Nouns: To help students identify and categorize nouns, remind them to ask themselves the following question: *Does this word name a person, a place, or a thing?* Before students begin their sentences, you may want to ask them to determine which nouns are singular and which are plural.

Let's Get Specific: Walk around the room to monitor students' progress. Have several thesauruses and dictionaries available for students to consult as they complete the web.

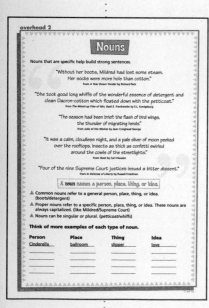

▲▲

▲ The Writing Connection

Which noun did students choose for the webs on their Let's Get Specific reproducible? Challenge them to write a short paragraph about this topic. The paragraph should include all the nouns in the web, as well as any others they can think of. Remind students to pay special attention to capitalizing proper nouns and deciding whether to use the singular or plural form of a noun.

▲ Keep in Mind

You may want to introduce students to the concept of concrete and abstract nouns. Concrete nouns, such as *horse* and *mitten*, are tangible and can be perceived by our senses. Abstract nouns, such as *honor* and *education* are intangible; we can't use our senses to perceive them. Explain to students that there are more concrete nouns than abstract nouns. Talk about why they think this is the case. Such a discussion can start students thinking about the nature of language and what it reveals about us.

Wanted by Sentences: Nouns

A noun names a person, place, thing, or idea.

Circle the nouns in the box.

skip	Mexico	pioneers	unhappy	where
freedom	lying	aroma	through	justice
cattle	speedily	wheels	Ruby	mountains

Sort the nouns you circled.

Person	Place	Thing
_____	_____	_____
_____	_____	_____
_____	_____	_____

Now use the nouns to write sentences.

1. Write a sentence about a person.

_____

2. Write a sentence about more than one person.

_____

3. Write a sentence about a thing.

_____

4. Write a sentence about more than one thing.

_____

5. Write a sentence about a place.

_____

6. Write a sentence about more than one place.

_____

Let's Get Specific

Using specific nouns can make your writing fresh and more interesting. A general noun like worker doesn't reveal much. Teacher, a more specific noun, gives you more information. An even more specific noun, such as Mr. Owens, presents a clearer picture of the teacher.

Underline the general noun in the sets of nouns below. Hint: Think about how that noun could be used as a heading for the other nouns in the set.

1. sneakers, boots, loafers, slippers, shoes, sandals

2. cotton, cloth, wool, rayon, silk, polyester, cashmere

3. fruit, plum, tangerine, apple, strawberry, watermelon

4. hammer, saw, screwdriver, ax, drill, tool

Good writers love searching for the perfect word. They often brainstorm to find just the right word.

Copy the web shown below on a sheet of paper. Write one of the nouns below in the center of the web. Complete it by adding more specific nouns. If you get stuck, consult a dictionary or a thesaurus.

bug   game   dessert   plant   illness

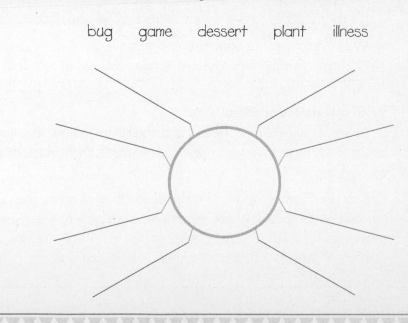

Pronouns

Overhead Transparency

◆ Pronouns

Reproducibles

◆ Call in the Pronouns!

◆ Problem Pronouns

◆ Pronouns Are so Agreeable

◆ Purpose ◆

To recognize pronouns and understand their function in sentences

Two common problems with pronoun usage crop up in student writing. First, pronoun usage can be vague because the antecedent is not clear. The second problem is faulty agreement when pronouns and their antecedents do not agree in number or gender.

▲ Launching Activity: Pronouns (Overhead 3)

As a volunteer reads aloud the first quote by William Steig, write the quote on the board but replace the pronouns with nouns. Ask the same volunteer to read aloud the quote you wrote. Encourage students to articulate which quote they think is clearer, and why. Discuss why the repetition of nouns can be unnecessary, confusing, and boring. At the end of the activity, have a volunteer read each quote and identify the pronoun(s) and antecedent(s).

Then review the information about pronouns on the overhead. To reinforce how crucial correct pronoun usage is, work on the exercises at the bottom of the overhead. Discuss why each sentence is confusing. Then have pairs of students work together to revise the sentences. Sample revisions appear below.

• In the backyard, Anna told her helper, "We will remove the tree limb because it is dead." (The original pronoun and verb did not agree in number with the antecedent.)

• As Anna paid for the puppy food, she looked at the chocolate chip cookie and thought how good it would taste. (The antecedent was unclear.)

• When Anna wanted something, she got it.
(The pronoun did not agree in gender with its antecedent.)

▲ Student Reproducibles

Since understanding pronouns and their antecedents can be a difficult concept to master, you may want to work on these reproducibles with the whole class.

Call in the Pronouns!: Review the definitions of *noun*, *pronoun*, and *antecedent*. In the last three sentences, students are asked to substitute pronouns for nouns. The last two sentences contain nouns of the same gender, so students need to be especially mindful about which nouns they

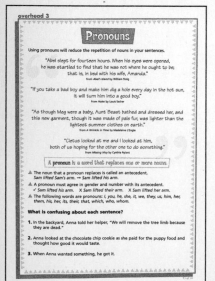

replace. Using too many pronouns can be as confusing and boring as using too many nouns, and this is especially true in sentence 5.

Problem Pronouns: Write the example on the board and then model the transformation to make sure students understand how the sentence was transformed by moving sections and changing some words.

Pronouns Are so Agreeable: Review the concepts of gender and number agreement before students begin this reproducible. To successfully complete this reproducible, students must be able to match each pronoun to its antecedent.

▲ The Writing Connection

Challenge students to write a short paragraph about their day—without using any pronouns. Have them skip lines so they can revise their work later. Ask volunteers to read aloud their work; hearing the constant repetition of nouns will soon cause students to realize the importance of pronouns. Then have them rewrite their paragraphs to include pronouns.

▲ Keep in Mind

Tracking pronoun antecedents is a critical reading skill. Many great writers use pronouns in a complex fashion or with intentional ambiguity. When Macbeth contemplates murdering the king, Shakespeare reveals the character's state of mind in part through pronoun usage; Macbeth repeatedly refers to regicide as "it," rather than calling regicide by name and having to face his intentions.

Call in the Pronouns!

Draw an arrow from each underlined pronoun to its antecedent. Circle the antecedent. For plural pronouns, you may have to circle more than one antecedent.

1. Prince loves stew, but <u>he</u> never eats the cooked carrots. Prince also refuses to eat dog chow because <u>he</u> hates <u>it</u> more than carrots. Beef stew and the occasional loaf of bread are Prince's preferred foods. For <u>him</u>, <u>these</u> make life worth living.

2. Carly put away the street map of <u>her</u> town. <u>She</u> kissed her poodle, Joe, on <u>his</u> head. Joe looked around, wondering if Carly was trying to map <u>his</u> backyard. <u>He</u> was only a dog, but <u>he</u> knew the location of every bone in the yard.

3. Serena, the cashier, thought the line at <u>her</u> register was too long. <u>She</u> stared at all the customers standing in line. <u>They</u> all looked very grumpy. Frowns covered <u>their</u> faces. Serena hoped it was almost time for <u>her</u> lunch break.

In the sentences below, which nouns should be replaced by pronouns? Underline the noun or nouns. Then write the appropriate pronouns above them.

4. One day Stephen was walking in Stephen's backyard when Stephen heard Rover bark. Although Rover liked Stephen, Rover was the sort of dog that Stephen hated.

5. Jessica liked to visit Jessica's cousin, Maribeth, during the summer because Maribeth had a pool that Jessica liked to swim in. Maribeth also baked homemade cookies whenever Jessica came to visit, and Jessica really liked Maribeth's cookies.

6. Jack couldn't believe how many DVDs Jack's friend Carl had. Carl used to work in a store that sold DVDs, and Carl's boss used to give Carl a discount on any DVDs Carl bought.

Problem Pronouns

Revise each sentence below to make its meaning clear. You may have to move sections of a sentence, repeat a noun, or add or change words.

Example:

Before: Sloppy Joe loved his old dog Susie almost as much as his mother, even though she had fleas.
Oops! Who has fleas—Sloppy Joe's dog or his mother?
After: Even though his old dog Susie had fleas, Sloppy Joe loved her as much as he loved his mother.

---

1. The doctor used a scalpel to operate on the heart, but then he left it in the operating room.

_____

_____

2. Eric hated cleaning the kitty litter box, and although he loved cleanliness, it made him sick.

_____

_____

3. When Shenikwa met her new step-grandparents, who were grilling hot dogs, the sight of them made her sick.

_____

_____

4. As Louis boarded Renata's ship, he thought she looked beautiful and kissed her.

_____

_____

5. In the orchard, Sandra picked apples and watched the workers making cider and she ate them.

_____

_____

Pronouns Are so Agreeable

**Correct the sentences so that each pronoun and its antecedent agree.
Write your corrections above the underlined pronouns.**

1. Thanksgiving was near, and turkeys everywhere had wisely decided <u>they</u> should be ignored.

2. The twins looked sweet, but <u>her</u> father knew <u>he</u> could get into trouble very easily.

3. Roberta put down her reading glasses, looked around the room, and then picked <u>it</u> up again.

4. Blanca made five peanut butter and jelly sandwiches for the picnic and then packed <u>it</u> in a basket.

5. Jeremy invited his friend Ilana to the races because he liked <u>them</u>.

Rewrite the sentences below to make the pronouns and their antecedents agree.

6. Her mother explained that cough drops were for colds and candy was for fun,
although it seemed like it was the same.

_____

_____

7. Jana thought one pair of socks was missing, but they found her inside the dryer.

_____

_____

8. Maggie stared at the apple and blueberry pies at the bakery
and hoped she could buy it for dessert.

_____

_____

Adjectives

◆ Purpose ◆

To understand the relationship between adjectives and nouns and to use adjectives more creatively

Many students often fall into the trap of repeatedly using bland adjectives. At the other end of the spectrum, exuberant young writers can also lean too heavily on adjectives. They think that if one or two adjectives are good, then even more adjectives must be better. As students think about including creative and powerful adjectives in their writing, they are learning to use language in a more meaningful way.

▲ Launching Activity: Adjectives (Overhead 4)

As you discuss the quotes on the overhead, have students identify the adjectives and the nouns they modify in each one. Then challenge them to be creative in choosing adjectives to complete the exercises at the bottom of the overhead. Use the questions to toss out a few adjectives to help get them started. *What kind of coyote is it? (lonely, limping, ravenous, mangy) How many coyotes are there? (one, lone, single) Which coyote is it? (this, that)* Encourage students to suggest more than one adjective, but remind them that each adjective should describe a different and distinct aspect of the noun. Really challenge them to use their imaginations to describe the nouns with vivid adjectives.

▲ Student Reproducibles

Adjective Action: As students complete the bottom of this reproducible, suggest they identify the noun that the adjective will modify. Also encourage them to brainstorm possible adjective choices on another sheet of paper.

Adjective Excellence: The focus here is that less is sometimes more when choosing adjectives. Set aside time for students to share the descriptions of their favorite places.

Combining Adjectives: In contrast to the overloaded sentences in Adjective Excellence, this reproducible focuses on short sentences that describe only one aspect of a noun. These aspects can often be combined into one sentence. After students complete the reproducible, have volunteers read aloud the original sentences and their revised sentences. Ask students which sentences were easier to read and to hear.

National Language Arts Standards:

▲ Uses adjectives in written compositions

▲ Uses grammatical and mechanical conventions in written compositions

Overhead Transparency

◆ Adjectives

Reproducibles

◆ Adjective Action

◆ Adjective Excellence

◆ Combining Adjectives

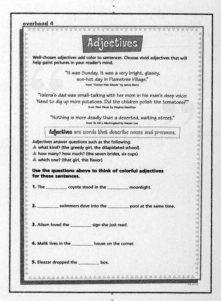

▲ The Writing Connection

Use unusual combinations of adjectives to trigger your students' imaginations. Give two slips of paper to each student. Ask them to write a noun on one strip and an adjective on the other strip. After collecting the strips, separate them into piles of nouns and adjectives and mix up the strips in each pile. (Quickly glance at the strips to weed out any untoward ideas.) Give one noun and one adjective to each student. These adjective-noun combinations will serve as the titles of descriptive, adjective-filled paragraphs. Students must find a way to make the title work, even if it's something like "The Shy Computer," but encourage creativity and coherence in their work. Have students write in pencil so they can underline and revise their adjective choices.

▲ Keep in Mind

By emphasizing the importance of adjective choice, you reinforce the importance of being thoughtful about every word choice. But be sure students understand that good writers go through several drafts before they are satisfied with their work. Creating successive drafts helps us rethink our writing choices, and writers can derive pleasure during the revision process. On the other hand, students shouldn't become obsessed with finding the right word when they write; good writing requires a delicate blend of control and letting go.

Adjective Action

Draw an arrow from each underlined adjective to the noun or pronoun it modifies.

1. The <u>fresh</u> breeze made the clothes on the line smell like sunshine.

2. The <u>sleek</u>, <u>blue</u> kayaks skimmed across the <u>pristine</u> lake.

3. Tardy students make teachers <u>unhappy</u>.

4. The <u>discarded</u> video no longer worked.

5. The <u>petite</u> girl enjoyed <u>sugary</u> treats.

Fill in each blank with an adjective. Avoid using overworked adjectives such as *good, bad, interesting, pretty, beautiful,* or *nice.*

6. After a _____ night, the _____ police officer went home and took a

   _____ shower.

7. _____ corn tastes wonderful on a _____ August day.

8. She left a _____ phone message about the _____ party.

9. The _____ television set seemed _____ once the new Harry Potter book arrived.

10. By _____ November, only the _____ candy was left in their Halloween pumpkin.

Adjective Excellence

Can a sentence contain too many adjectives? You bet! Underline the adjectives below that are too similar. Then rewrite each sentence with fewer adjectives to make it stronger.

1. The loud, roaring, noisy, coughing lawn mower woke up the sleepy, talented, wonderful, exhausted student on Saturday morning.

_____

_____

Read each pair of sentences. Circle the sentence that uses adjectives well.

2. A. The girl in the photograph looked pretty, beautiful, and gorgeous.
    B. The night, cold and quiet, settled around the house.

3. A. Thick and creamy chocolate frosting covered the cake.
    B. Sasha thought the new teacher was nice and kind.

4. A. The metallic silver car glinted in the hot sun.
    B. That bird was bright yellow.

5. A. The wonderful, terrific season of intoxicating, thrilling baseball was upon them.
    B. Wispy fog drifted across the lake's still surface.

6. What is your favorite place? How would you describe it? On the back of this sheet, list at least ten adjectives to describe the place. Use your senses: How does it look? What do you hear when you're there? Include <u>too many</u> of your adjectives in a sentence. Then rewrite the sentence on the lines below. Choose your adjectives carefully to create the feeling of the place.

_____

_____

_____

_____

Name _____   Date _____

Combining Adjectives

Unnecessary repetition in sentences can try the patience of readers. Short, related sentences containing adjectives can often be combined to form one sentence.

Example:
Before: The suspension bridge was steel. It stretched high above the Rio Grande. It was old.
After: The old steel suspension bridge stretched high above the Rio Grande.

Word order can affect the meaning of a sentence. Depending on what you want to say, you can combine sentences in different ways.

Combine each set of sentences into one sentence.

1. The bees were industrious. They were sweat bees. They were tiny.

_____

_____

2. Maine's Peacock Beach State Park covers 100 acres. It has a small beach. It has a swimming area.

_____

_____

3. Oregon is a coastal state. It is rainy. It is also very lush. It is very green.

_____

_____

4. The homework was difficult. It was time consuming. It was Latin homework.

_____

_____

5. The Fourth of July was humid. There were few fireworks on the Fourth of July. The Fourth of July was stormy.

_____

_____

National Language Arts Standards:

▲ Uses verbs in written composition

▲ Uses a wide variety of action verbs

▲▲▲▲▲▲▲▲▲▲▲▲▲▲▲▲

Overhead Transparency

◆ Verbs

Reproducibles

◆ I Am so Tense!

◆ Action Heroes

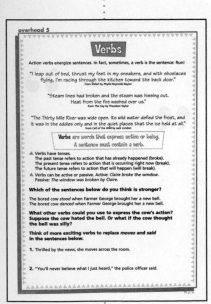

Verbs

◆ Purpose ◆

To understand the role of verbs in sentences and to utilize a variety of verbs in writing

Verbs bring sentences to life. The subject of a sentence may be understood, but a verb can never be taken for granted. *Sal!* is an exclamation or a greeting, but it's not a sentence. We have no idea what Sal is doing. *Shout!* is a sentence. If there is no verb, there is no sentence. Playing with a variety of verbs allows students to see how the alteration of a word can change the tone and intent of a sentence.

▲ Launching Activity: Verbs (Overhead 5)

Begin by discussing students' reactions to the quotes on the overhead and how the writers used verbs. Then go over the information about verbs. You might find that a brief discussion of linking and helping verbs will help students better understand the passive voice. You can review regular and irregular verbs here or wait until students tackle the I Am so Tense! reproducible.

As students debate which of the sentences about the cow and the bell is stronger, guide them in seeing how the meaning and tone of the sentence changed with each verb. The second sentence is stronger because it gives the impression that the cow is excited about receiving the bell. The cow's action in the first sentence is vague. She may be curious, she may be excited, or she may always stand when the farmer walks in. To invigorate students' verb suggestions, encourage them to close their eyes and imagine the cow as a character rather than a real animal.

To wrap up the activity, challenge students to think of as many different synonyms for the words *moves* and *said* as they can. List the synonyms on the board. Some examples are shown below.

Moves: *skips, runs, jumps, hops, scuttles, dances, walks, leaps, hurries, stumbles*

Said: *spoke, whispered, shouted, explained, murmured, hollered, muttered*

▲ Student Reproducibles

I Am so Tense!: Before students begin this reproducible, designate half the class as past tense and the other half as future tense. Call out a series of regular and irregular verbs in the present tense, and have groups supply the past and future tenses. Remind them to look for regular verbs ending in –*ed* to identify the past tense and the word *will* to identify the future tense.

Action Heroes: Make sure students understand the difference between active and passive voice. Tell them to think about whether the subject of the sentence is doing the action (active) or is receiving the action (passive). Sentences written in the active voice are much livelier and engaging than those written in the passive voice. Point out that each passive voice verb phrase contains a helping verb such as *is* or *was* combined with an action verb.

▲ The Reading Connection

To open students to the possibilities of verbs, have them start their own verb collections. As students read, remind them to pay special attention to the verbs the writers use and to write down their favorites. Set aside time each week for them to share the additions to their collections. Also encourage students to incorporate these new verbs into their own writing. Students will find that they can become quite creative and bold in the verbs they use.

I Am so Tense!

Underline the verb in each sentence. Then identify the tense.

Example: The kitten ____batted____ the ball with its paws. ____past____

1. Because of the wind, Jed anchored his map with a rock. _____

2. We will depart on our vacation tomorrow morning. _____

3. The speedboat jetted past our sailboat. _____

4. A seagull snatches a bite of Alex's tuna sandwich. _____

5. Leah caught an enormous fish in the cove. _____

Complete the sets of sentences below. Write the sentences using the proper tense of the verb.

6. Past: The deep-sea diver balanced on the side of the boat.

Present: The deep-sea diver balances on the side of the boat.

Future: _____

7. Past: Gordon lost a pearl in the sand.

Present: _____

Future: Gordon will lose a pearl in the sand.

8. Past: _____

Present: _____

Future: A grain of sand inside an oyster will turn into a pearl.

Action Heroes

In your own writing, try to use more active voice sentences than passive voice ones. Too many sentences written in the passive voice will make your writing seem dull.

Active Voice: *The teacher handed out the test.*
The subject, teacher, does the action.

Passive Voice: *The test was handed out by the teacher.*
The action is happening to the subject, test.

Rewrite each sentence to make the verb active.

1. In the summer, Fifi is clipped by the veterinarian.

_____

_____

2. Fifi's brown eyes were hidden by her long white eyebrows.

_____

_____

3. Now she is blinded by the brilliant yellow sunshine.

_____

_____

4. Several pairs of canine sunglasses were tried on by Fifi.

_____

_____

5. A pair of bright red sunglasses was bought for Fifi by her owner, Lisa.

_____

_____

Adverbs

National Language
Arts Standards:

▲ Uses adverbs in
written composition

▲ Chooses between
forms of adjectives
and adverbs

**Overhead
Transparency**

◆ Adverbs

Reproducibles

◆ Adverb Action

◆ Adverb or
Adjective?

◆ Strengthen
Sentences With
Adverbs and
Adjectives

◆ Purpose ◆

To recognize adverbs and to avoid common problems in adverb usage

Learning to incorporate adverbs into their writing presents a number of challenges to students. Those who have learned the "adverbs end in –ly" rule can become confused since many adverbs don't follow this rule. Another problem students encounter is difficulty in distinguishing between adverbs and adjectives. And finally, some students tend to overuse the same adverbs.

▲ Launching Activity: Adverbs (Overhead 6)

Before introducing adverbs, you may want to display the Adjectives overhead as a review. Remind students that adjectives modify nouns and pronouns. Then you can segue logically into introducing adverbs as words that modify verbs, adjectives, and other adverbs.

Remind students to ask the following series of questions to distinguish between adverbs and adjectives:

• Which word is being modified?

• What part of speech is that word?

• Is the word a verb, an adjective, or an adverb? If so, the modifier is an adverb. Is the word a noun or pronoun? If so, the modifier is an adjective.

Then model how you would identify the adverbs and the words they modify in the first quote: *I see that the word* calmly *modifies the word* replied, *which is a verb. I can ask myself, "How did Mama's voice reply? Calmly." I know that calmly is an adverb. It also ends in –ly, an ending that often signals an adverb.* Then let students take over the process.

Guide students in identifying the adverbs and adjectives in the exercises at the bottom of the overhead: 1. adverb: *really* modifies *strange* (adj.) 2. adjective: *real* modifies *lemonade* (noun) 3. adverb: *late* modifies *arrived* (verb) 4. adjective: *enormous* modifies *meal* (noun); adverb: *vigorously* modifies *walked* (verb)

▲ Student Reproducibles

Adverb Action: Model a partial answer to the first sentence: *In her cupcakes, the baker* <u>*always*</u> *uses the* <u>*very*</u> *best chocolate.* The verb in this sentence is *uses. The adverb* always *tells me how often the baker* uses *that chocolate. In this sentence,* always *modifies the verb* uses. Then have students complete this first set of sentences on their own. For the second set of sentences, encourage students to be creative in their use of adverbs.

Adverb or Adjective?: Note that the third sentence can be correct with either the adjective or the adverb: *Cleverly, Sherlock Holmes solved the mystery./Clever Sherlock Holmes solved the mystery.* Make sure students recognize which word(s) the adjective and adverb modify. Before students begin writing their own sentences, remind them that each of the words in the box can be used as an adverb or adjective, depending upon the word or words it modifies.

Strengthen Sentences With Adverbs and Adjectives: In this reproducible, students are basically revising a story and making it more lively and interesting by adding adverbs and adjectives. Before students begin, have them write down their own additions to the example sentence, *The puppet dances.* As they share their newly elaborated sentences, point out how these changes made the sentences stronger by making them more descriptive.

▲ The Reading Connection

Create an Adventures in Adverbs bulletin board. Write the definition of an adverb at the top. Staple construction-paper pockets to the board with the titles HOW? WHEN? WHERE? HOW OFTEN? Ask students to look for adverbs as they read. Have them copy down sentences with adverbs that they particularly like and then file them in the correct pocket on the bulletin board. Set aside time to share the contents of the pockets.

Adverb Action

Draw an arrow from the underlined adverbs to the words they modify.

1. In her cupcakes, the baker always uses the <u>very</u> best chocolate.

2. <u>Sometimes</u> the children longed to take naps.

3. Max was <u>so</u> eager that he dropped the plate.

4. Bats can hear <u>extremely</u> well in the dark.

5. The snow fell <u>lazily</u> and <u>peacefully</u> in the forest.

Think of different adverbs and adverb phrases to complete each sentence. Use an adverb or adverb phrase that answers each question.

> *Example:* Tori threw the softball _____.
> How? Tori threw the softball ___hard___.
> When? Tori threw the softball _yesterday_.
> Where? Tori threw the softball ___away___.
> How often? Tori threw the softball ___rarely___.

6. Marion ran _____.

How? _____

When? _____

Where? _____

How often? _____

7. On the shuttle, the astronauts read the instruments _____.

How? _____

When? _____

Where? _____

How often? _____

Adverb or Adjective?

It's important to be able to tell the difference between an adverb and an adjective so you can use them correctly in your writing. Remember to look at the word being modified. Adverbs modify verbs, adjectives, and other adverbs. Adjectives modify nouns and pronouns.

Read each sentence below. Does the underlined adverb or adjective belong in it? Circle the correct word. Then try reading aloud the sentence to hear how each word sounds.

1. The donkey sauntered <u>slow/slowly</u> down the hill.

2. Opening the lock was <u>difficult/difficulty</u> to do.

3. <u>Clever/Cleverly</u> Sherlock Holmes solved the mystery.

4. <u>Sweet/Sweetly</u> honey can be found in beehives.

5. After her <u>clumsy/clumsily</u> performance, Kris walked home <u>silent/silently</u>.

Not all adverbs end in –ly. Write sentences using the words in the box as adverbs.

first	south	fast	inside	late

6. _____

7. _____

8. _____

9. _____

10. _____

Strengthen Sentences With Adverbs and Adjectives

Modifying a simple sentence with adverbs and adjectives can make the sentence clearer and more interesting.

Add adverbs and adjectives to the sentences below. Insert a caret (^) to show where you want to add the modifiers.

graceful wooden   easily
Example: The ^ puppet dances ^.

1. The toy maker dozed and began to snore.

2. Moonlight flowed through windows and filled corners of the shop.

3. Pieces of the dollhouse floated over the table.

4. A spoon danced with a fork.

5. Raggedy Ann sang a song, while Teddy Bear practiced steps.

6. A ladybug hopped on the toy maker's nose.

7. She sneezed and woke herself up.

8. The toy maker went back to work.

Prepositions & Conjunctions

◆ Purpose ◆

To introduce prepositional phrases and conjunctions

National Language Arts Standards:

▲ Uses prepositions in written compositions

▲ Uses coordinating conjunctions in written compositions

Learning how to use prepositional phrases and conjunctions will help students incorporate a variety of sentence styles into their writing. Prepositional phrases offer writers a way of beginning sentences with something other than subjects. When students use conjunctions, they can build more complex sentences that flow more smoothly than a series of short, choppy sentences.

▲ Launching Activity: Prepositions & Conjunctions (Overhead 7)

Before beginning this lesson, prepare separate lists of prepositions and coordinating conjunctions for students to refer to as necessary. In discussing the quotes on the reproducible, ask students to identify the prepositions and conjunctions and how they contribute variety to the writing.

To allow students to focus independently on each part of speech, divide this lesson into two parts and present them on different days. As you go over the prepositions, ask students whether each prepositional phrase is being used as an adjective or an adverb, and which words the phrase is modifying. Remind them to ask questions to identify adjectives and adverbs (for adjectives, *what kind*, *how many*, *which one*; for adverbs: *how*, *where*, *when*, *how often*). Discuss the phrase's location in the sentence, and whether or not it could be moved. Emphasize the use of the objective pronouns in the second sentence.

When discussing conjunctions, point out that Beverly Cleary used two different conjunctions in her sentence. To demonstrate how conjunctions link words—and help writers avoid repetition—rewrite the first sentence in the exercise as two sentences: *Texas borders Mexico. New Mexico borders Mexico.* Then ask students to take away the conjunction in the second sentence and rewrite it as two sentences.

Answers for the overhead: Prepositions 1. with fear, beside the garbage can 2. At dinner/of potatoes/between my sister and me; Conjunctions 1. and; Texas, New Mexico (subjects) 2. but; I live in Texas, I have never visited Mexico (sentences)

▲▲▲▲▲▲▲▲▲▲▲▲

Overhead Transparency

◆ Prepositions & Conjunctions

Reproducibles

◆ Prepositions on the Move

◆ Conjunction Connection

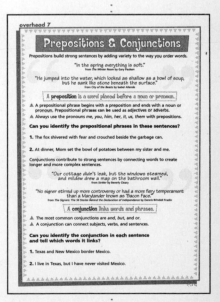

▲ Student Reproducibles

Prepositions on the Move: The key here is to show students that prepositional phrases can occur in different places in a sentence. However, they need to become aware of when the placement of a phrase makes a sentence confusing or awkward. Explain that an adverbial phrase can more easily be moved around in a sentence, while an adjectival phrase must remain close to the noun or pronoun it modifies. In sentence 4, make sure students understand that *on beds* modifies the verb *sun, of broken branches* modifies the noun *beds*—which is part of a prepositional phrase itself—and *above the ground* modifies the verb *sun*.

Conjunction Connection: Write nouns such as *peas* and *carrots* on the board, and model your own sentences to remind students that nouns can be used as subjects, direct objects, and objects of prepositions: *Peas or carrots is a good choice for dinner. My father nestled peas and carrots on his sandwich. The bunny piled peas and carrots in the basket. The parrot eats peas but not carrots.*

▲ The Reading Connection

Challenge students to go on a Preposition and Conjunction Hunt as they read. They can store their results in envelopes, containers, or notebooks at a writing and/or reading center.

▲ Keep in Mind

Students—and adults—often err in using the correct form of a pronoun with a preposition. Objective pronouns always follow prepositions: *between you and me* is correct, while *between you and I* is not.

Another problem is the usage of *between* and *among: between* is used with two people or things; *among* is used with more than two people or things. Remind students, too, that *off* should not be followed by of: *He took his coat off the hook* is correct. *He took his coat off of the hook* is not.

Prepositions on the Move

Underline all of the prepositional phrases in each sentence. Tell whether the phrase is an adjective or an adverb phrase. Then decide which phrases you can move to make the sentences more interesting. Rewrite those sentences.

1. You would find sun bears in the tropical rainforests of Southeast Asia.

_____

2. Sun bears are the smallest species of bear.

_____

3. These bears enjoy resting or sunbathing during the day.

_____

4. They sun themselves on beds of broken branches above the ground.

_____

The location of some prepositional phrases makes the sentences below totally confusing. Underline the prepositional phrases. Then move them to create clearer and stronger sentences.

5. Jacques, the lifeguard, warned Heather to stop swimming in French.

_____

6. Heather kept swimming from America because she didn't speak French across the pool.

_____

7. To Heather, finally, Jacques jumped and swam into the water.

_____

8. In the air, Jacques touched Jolene's shoulder out of breath, and Jolene jumped.

_____

Conjunction Connection

**Use the conjunctions *and*, *or*, or *but* to combine the following words.
Then write a sentence for each combination.**

1.

Selena		Stella

_____

2.

lumbered		stumbled

_____

3.

out of the yard		into the air

_____

4.

created a mess		was beautiful

_____

5.

Santa Fe	Austin	Phoenix

_____

Participles

◆ Purpose ◆

To identify participles and understand how to use them as modifiers

Acquainting students with participles and participial phrases will expand their understanding of how to extend sentences to create greater variety in their writing. Learning about misplaced modifiers will strengthen students' grasp of sentence logic and help them begin to see word groups rather than words in isolation.

National Language Arts Standards:

▲ Uses a variety of sentence structures to expand and embed ideas

Overhead Transparency

◆ Participles

Reproducibles

◆ Participle Hunt

◆ Modifiers on the Loose

▲ Launching Activity: Participles (Overhead 8)

Students often confuse participles and gerunds. They can also fail to distinguish between participles that are adjectives and participles that are part of a verb phrase. Review the differences as necessary with students.

- Participles and participial phrases act as adjectives.
  (The purring cat is happy. Purring in the sun, the cat seemed happy.)

- A participle linked with a helping verb acts as a verb.
  (The happy cat is purring.)

- Gerunds end in –ing and act as nouns. (Purring means that a cat is happy.)

Discuss the participles in the quotes. If no one mentions it, point out the different position of each participial phrase. Talk about how the placement affects the structure of each sentence. Then go over the exercises at the bottom of the overhead. The answers are: 1. verb 2. participle *screaming* modifies *Liz* 3. participle *stretched* modifies *hose* 4. verbs

▲ Student Reproducibles

Participle Hunt: Remind students that participles are verb forms used as adjectives. Be on the lookout for students who have trouble recognizing past participles that end in *t, en,* or *n.* Have pairs of students exchange story endings and identify the participles and what they modify.

Modifiers on the Loose: Work through the example with students. Ask them which noun the participial phrase is modifying, *Suzanne* or *corner.* If necessary, remind students to ask themselves who or what waited at the corner. Also, be sure to point out that introductory participial phrases are set off by commas.

▲ The Writing Connection

Ask students to complete a sentence that begins with a participial phrase, such as *Tramping through the knee-deep snow, . . .* or *Holding twenty balloons in one hand, ...* After reviewing their sentences, challenge students to use the sentences as the beginning of a short short story.

Participle Hunt

Read the story.

      The <u>tattered</u> sign on the pole said the missing cat's name was Participle. Participle! Babe thought. What a strange name for a cat! Feeling sad for Participle's owner, Babe copied down the description of the cat. It had gray eyes and short gray fur, and a bent tail.

      A few days later, Babe was sitting on her front porch and watching birds. Suddenly, the mockingbirds and sparrows splashing in the birdbath scattered. Babe saw a flash of gray out of the corner of her eye. Wondering whether she had seen a mourning dove or a lost cat, Babe called softly, "Participle, is that you?"

      A loud meow! came from the bushes.

The first participle in the story is underlined. Find and underline the rest of the participles. Then complete the chart below.

Participle	Past or Present?	Modifies
tattered	past	sign
_____	_____	_____
_____	_____	_____
_____	_____	_____
_____	_____	_____
_____	_____	_____
_____	_____	_____
_____	_____	_____

Has Participle been found? Complete the story on back of this page—and be sure to include participles in your ending.

Modifiers on the Loose

The participial phrases in these sentences are in the wrong places. Identify which nouns or pronouns the phrases are modifying. Then rewrite the sentences to move the phrases closer to the words they're modifying.

> *Example:* Suzanne waited at the corner <u>hoping to see the parade</u>.
> <u>Hoping to see the parade</u>, Suzanne waited at the corner.

1. Clowns came by on stilts pretending to sweep the street.

_____

2. Burnt by the sun, a shiny red fire engine carried firefighters.

_____

3. Bicyclists, riding on a float, pedaled in front of the Corn Queen.

_____

4. The queen threw popcorn to the crowd popped that morning.

_____

5. A group of children marched after the float dressed like ears of corn.

_____

6. At the end of the parade, riding a camel, Suzanne spotted Mayor Hurley.

_____

Choose one of the participial phrases in the box. Include the phrase in at least three sentences. Put the participial phrase in a different place in each sentence. Then ask a partner to find the the word the phrase modifies.

excited by the crowd	returning to the scene	frightened by the roar

7. _____

8. _____

9. _____

Subject-Verb Agreement

◆ Purpose ◆

To identify subjects and understand subject-verb agreement

National Language Arts Standards:

▲ Uses verbs in written compositions

▲ Uses verbs that agree with the subject

Being able to identify the subject of a sentence is crucial to understanding sentence structure and remedying common writing problems such as errors with subject-verb agreement. Even high school students have trouble with agreement, especially when modifying, interruptive phrases separate the subject and verb. Although the exercises on the overhead and reproducibles simplify the topic, they will help students become more familiar with the concept of agreement and provide practice for solving common errors.

▲ Launching Activity: Subject-Verb Agreement (Overhead 9)

Before displaying the overhead, you may want to review the concept of singular and plural nouns and verbs. Sometimes even the most capable students need to review basic rules. Then call on volunteers to read aloud the quotes on the overhead. After going over the information about subject-verb agreement, ask students to identify the subjects and verbs in the quotes. Discuss how they ascertained whether the subjects and verbs were singular or plural. For the exercises at the bottom of the overhead, you may want students to read aloud each sentence with both verb choices so they can hear the difference when the subject and verb don't agree. Answers: 1. is 2. was 3. likes 4. are 5. have 6. were

Overhead Transparency

◆ Subject-Verb Agreement

Reproducibles

◆ What Is This all About?

◆ We're in Complete Agreement

◆ Subjects and Verbs Tragically Separated

▲ Student Reproducibles

What Is This all About?: Go over the first exercise in each section with students. Point out that the subject in exercise 1 is *people*, not *some people*. Remind students that subjects are nouns or pronouns; modifying adjectives should be not be written down.

We're in Complete Agreement: Let pairs of students work together on this reproducible. Have one identify the subject and tell whether it is singular or plural while the other selects the correct verb. Ask them to collaborate on writing the two sentences.

Subjects and Verbs Tragically Separated: Since interruptive phrases can be quite confusing, work on this reproducible with students. Make sure they are able to identify the subject, the verb, and the interruptive phrase.

Remind them that a sentence should still make sense after the phrase has been removed. The phrase is a detail that enhances the meaning, but it is not essential to the sentence. Also point out that in sentences 1 and 7, two interruptive phrases, a participial and a prepositional, are joined together. Both must be placed within parentheses.

▲ The Writing Connection

Have groups of four or five students create their own sentences with interruptive phrases. After one member writes down a subject, all of the other members—except the last one—contribute an interruptive phrase. The last member must read over the sentence and supply the correct form of a verb. Continue the activity until every student has contributed a subject, phrases, and a verb.

▲ Keep in Mind

Learning to recognize and use interruptive phrases exposes students to the complexities of the English language. Writers such as Shakespeare, William Faulkner, and Toni Morrison achieve amazing effects with the use of sustained interruptive phrases in their work.

What Is This all About?

Answer the question to find the subject of each sentence.

1. Some people call Elvis Presley the King of Rock and Roll.

Question: **Who** calls Elvis Presley the King of Rock and Roll?

Answer: _____

2. Elvis lived in a mansion that he named Graceland.

Question: **Who** lived in a mansion that he named Graceland?

Answer: _____

3. Fried peanut butter and banana sandwiches were Elvis's favorite snack.

Question: **What** was Elvis's favorite snack?

Answer: _____

4. For fourteen years, Mary Jenkins Langston cooked for Elvis at Graceland.

Question: **Who** cooked for Elvis at Graceland?

Answer: _____

Now it's your turn to write a question about the subject—and answer it.

5. Elvis always wanted his food prepared quickly.

Question: _____

Answer: _____

6. Biscuits, eggs, bacon, and sausage were part of Elvis's huge breakfasts.

Question: _____

Answer: _____

7. One time, when Elvis was in the hospital, the doctors placed him on a special diet.

Question: _____

Answer: _____

8. Without the doctors' knowledge, Ms. Langston smuggled hot dogs into the hospital for Elvis.

Question: _____

Answer: _____

We're in Complete Agreement

Remember that the subject and verb of a sentence must be in complete agreement. A subject that is singular refers to one person or thing. A singular subject takes a singular verb.

Venus Williams **plays** in tennis tournaments frequently.

A subject that is plural refers to more than one person or thing. A plural subject takes a plural verb.

Venus and Serena Williams **play** in tennis tournaments around the world.

Underline the subject of each sentence. Decide whether it is singular or plural. Then circle the correct form of the verb.

1. The Williams sisters (has played/have played) tennis since they were four.

2. Today, they (is/are) among the best tennis players in the world.

3. Both sisters (hits/hit) the ball extremely hard.

4. This (makes/make) it difficult for the other player to hit the ball back.

5. Off the tennis court, Serena (surfs/surf) and (skateboards/skateboard).

6. Venus's biography (reveals/reveal) that blue (is/are) her favorite color.

7. Venus (is/are) taller than her sister and (weighs/weigh) more.

8. Neither sister (enjoys/enjoy) watching scary movies.

Now it's your turn to write some sentences.

9. Write a sentence that has the subject *Nathan and his dog.*

_____

10. Write a sentence that has the verb *scoot.*

_____

Subjects and Verbs Tragically Separated

Sometimes a phrase separates the subject and verb. The verb must still agree with the subject of the sentence— and not with the noun or pronoun in the phrase. To find the subject, think of the sentence without the phrase.

The coyotes on the prairie howl all night long.

subject	phrase	verb	
The coyotes	(on the prairie)	howl	all night long.

The coyotes howl all night long.

Underline the subject. Place parentheses around the phrase that separates the subject and verb. Then circle the correct form of the verb.

1. The man wearing the stack of purple hats (look/looks) silly.

2. Afternoons on the Great Plains (gets/get) hot.

3. People who spend a lot of time outdoors (protect/protects) themselves.

4. None of them (is/are) foolish enough to leave a purple hat at home.

5. In the spring, hundreds of wildflowers (dots/dot) the prairie.

6. Butterflies of every type (floats/float) across the tall grasses.

7. Children smearing sunscreen on their noses (watches/watch) the butterflies.

8. A woman with two cameras (snaps/snap) pictures of the children.

Sentence Fragments & Run-ons

National Language
Arts Standards:

▲ Uses a variety of
sentence structures
to expand and
embed ideas

▲ Uses nouns and verbs
in written compositions

▲ Uses conventions of
punctuation in written
compositions

◆ Purpose ◆

To recognize sentence fragments and run-on sentences and how to correct them

entence fragments and run-on sentences sometimes result when students write too quickly and don't go back to proofread their work.

Overhead Transparency

◆ Sentence Fragments & Run-ons

Reproducible

◆ Sentence Detective

▲ Launching Activity: Sentence Fragments & Run-ons (Overhead 10)

As evidenced in the fiction quotes on the overhead, students are likely to encounter sentence fragments and run-on sentences in the work of well-known authors. Help students understand why these writers used incomplete sentences or run-ons: The writer may have wanted to emphasize a particular point with a fragment or show stream-of-consciousness with run-ons. Emphasize that a writer must be experienced and have a full understanding of grammar and sentence logic to pull this off successfully. Have students rewrite the introductory sentences on the overhead to make them complete. (1, 3, and 4 are run-on sentences; 2 is a fragment.)

▲ Student Reproducible

Sentence Detective: Remind students to look for both a subject and a verb in the sentences. In a sentence with more than one subject and verb and no coordinating conjunction, they should focus on whether the sentence expresses more than one thought and should be broken into two or more sentences.

▲ The Writing Connection

Set up a collection of story starters using theme- or genre-based sentence fragments and run-on sentences. Place the starters in labeled envelopes such as LOVE, GREED, LOYALTY, or REALISTIC FICTION, SCIENCE FICTION, HISTORICAL FICTION, FAIRY TALES, FOLK TALES, NON-FICTION, and so on. After selecting a story starter and rewriting it as a complete sentence or two sentences, students can begin their stories or articles.

Sentence Detective

Can you detect which of these sentences are complete and which are fragments or run-ons? Rewrite sentence fragments and run-on sentences to make them correct.

1. Cheetahs are the fastest animals on earth and can run seventy miles per hour.

_____

2. Both lions and hyenas run swiftly across the plains.

_____

3. Cheetahs reach speeds of seventy miles per hour, chickens run nine miles per hour.

_____

4. Giant tortoises slow moving.

_____

5. Perhaps because their legs are short, pigs eleven miles per hour.

_____

6. Cheetahs are the fastest animals, garden snails are the slowest.

_____

7. An elk's speed is 45 miles per hour, but an elephant can travel at 25 miles an hour.

_____

8. The average speeds of wart hogs, grizzly bears, and white-tailed deer are about the same.

_____

Answer Key

Page 7 Pick the Stronger Sentence

1. B
2. A
3. A
4. B
5. A

Page 10 Wanted by Sentences: Nouns

Person: pioneers, Ruby; Place: Mexico, mountains; Thing: freedom, aroma, justice, cattle, wheels. 1–6: Sentences will vary.

Page 11 Let's Get Specific

1. shoes
2. cloth
3. fruit
4. tool

Answers on web will vary.

Page 14 Call in the Pronouns!

1. Prince loves stew, but he never eats the cooked carrots. Prince also refuses to eat dog chow because he hates it more than carrots. Beef stew and the occasional loaf of bread are Prince's preferred foods. For him, these make life worth living.

2. Carly put away the street map of her town. She kissed her poodle, Joe, on his head. Joe looked around, wondering if Carly was trying to map his backyard. He was only a dog, but he knew the location of every bone in the yard.

3. Serena, the cashier, thought the line at her register was too long. She stared at all the customers standing in line. They all looked very grumpy. Frowns covered their faces. Serena hoped it was almost time for her lunch break.

4. One day Stephen was walking in his backyard when he heard Rover bark. Although Rover liked Stephen, Rover was the sort of dog that Stephen hated.

5. Jessica liked to visit her cousin, Maribeth, during the summer because Maribeth had a pool that Jessica liked to swim in. Maribeth also baked homemade cookies whenever Jessica came to visit, and Jessica really liked her cookies.

6. Jack couldn't believe how many DVDs his friend Carl had. Carl used to work in a store that sold DVDs, and his boss used to give him a discount on any DVDs he bought.

Page 15 Problem Pronouns

1. The doctor used a scalpel to operate on the heart, but then he left the scalpel in the operating room.

2. Although Eric loved cleanliness, he hated cleaning the kitty litter box because it made him sick.

3. When Shenikwa met her new step-grandparents, who were grilling hot dogs, the sight of the food made her sick.

4. As Louis boarded Renata's ship, he thought Renata looked beautiful and kissed her.

5. In the orchard, Sandra picked apples and ate them as she watched the workers making cider.

Page 16 Pronouns Are so Agreeable

1. Thanksgiving was near, and turkeys everywhere had wisely decided they [it] should be ignored.

2. The twins looked sweet, but her [their] father knew he [they] could get into trouble very easily.

3. Roberta put down her reading glasses, looked around the room, and then picked it [them] up again.

4. Blanca made five peanut butter and jelly sandwiches for the picnic and then packed it [them] in a basket.

5. Jeremy invited his friend Ilana to the races because he liked them [her].

6. Her mother explained that cough drops were for colds and candy was for fun, although it seemed like they were the same.

7. Jana thought one pair of socks was missing, but she found them inside the dryer.

8. Maggie stared at the apple and blueberry pies at the bakery and hoped she could buy them for dessert.

Page 19 Adjective Action

1. The fresh breeze made the clothes on the line smell like sunshine.

2. The sleek, blue kayaks skimmed across the pristine lake.

3. Tardy students make teachers unhappy.

4. The discarded video no longer worked.

5. The petite girl enjoyed sugary treats.

Possible answers:

6. After a hectic night, the exhausted police officer went home and took a long, hot shower.

7. Buttery corn tastes wonderful on a sweltering August day.

8. She left a rambling phone message about the fiftieth-wedding-anniversary party.

9. The flat screen television set seemed inconsequential once the new Harry Potter book arrived.

10. By early November, only the smashed candy was left in their Halloween pumpkin.

Page 20 Adjective Excellence

1. Possible answer: The roaring and coughing lawnmower woke up the talented but exhausted student on Saturday morning.

2. B.

3. A.

4. A.

5. B.

6. *Answers will vary.*

Page 21 Combining Adjectives

1. The tiny sweat bees were industrious.

2. Maine's Peacock Beach State Park covers 100 acres, and it has a small beach and a swimming area.

3. A rainy coastal state, Oregon is very lush and green.

4. The Latin homework was difficult and time consuming.

5. The Fourth of July was humid and stormy so there were few fireworks.

Page 24 I Am so Tense!

1. Because of the wind, Jed <u>anchored</u> his map with a rock. [past]

2. We <u>will depart</u> on our vacation tomorrow morning. [future]

3. The speedboat <u>jetted</u> past our sailboat. [past]

4. A seagull <u>snatches</u> a bite of Alex's tuna sandwich. [present]

5. Leah <u>caught</u> an enormous fish in the cove. [past]

6. Future: <u>The deep-sea diver will balance on the side of the boat.</u>

7. Present: <u>Gordon loses a pearl in the sand</u>.

8. Past: <u>A grain of sand inside an oyster turned into a pearl.</u>

   Present: <u>A grain of sand inside an oyster turns into a pearl.</u>

Page 25 Action Heroes

1. In the summer, the veterinarian clips Fifi.

2. Fifi's long white eyebrows hid her brown eyes.

3. Now the brilliant yellow sunshine blinds her.

4. Fifi tried on several pairs of canine sunglasses.

5. Fifi's owner, Lisa, bought a pair of bright red sunglasses for Fifi.

Page 28 Adverb Action

1. In her cupcakes, the baker always uses the <u>very</u> best chocolate.

2. <u>Sometimes</u> the children longed to take naps.

3. Max was <u>so</u> eager that he dropped the plate.

4. Bats can hear <u>extremely</u> well in the dark.

5. The snow fell <u>lazily</u> and <u>peacefully</u> in the forest.

6. Marion ran <u>fast</u>.

Marion ran <u>yesterday</u>.

Marion ran <u>by the river</u>.

Marion ran <u>often</u>.

7. On the shuttle, the astronauts read the instruments <u>with care</u>.

On the shuttle, the astronauts read the instruments <u>on the hour</u>.

On the shuttle, the astronauts read the instruments <u>on the control panel</u>.

On the shuttle, the astronauts read the instruments <u>frequently</u>.

Page 29 Adverb or Adjective?

1. slowly

2. difficult

3. Clever or Cleverly

4. Sweet

5. clumsy; silently

6–10. *Sentences will vary.*

Page 30 Strengthen Sentences With Adverbs and Adjectives

Answers will vary.

Page 33 Prepositions on the Move

1. You would find sun bears <u>in the tropical rainforests</u> of Southeast Asia. [adverbs]

   In the tropical rainforests of Southeast Asia, you would find sun bears.

2. Sun bears are the smallest species <u>of bear</u>. [adjective]

3. These bears enjoy resting or sunbathing <u>during the day</u>. [adverb]

   During the day, these bears enjoy resting or sunbathing.

4. They sun themselves <u>on beds</u> <u>of broken branches</u> <u>above the ground</u>. [adverb/adjective/adverb]

   Above the ground on beds of broken branches, they sun themselves.

5. In French, Jacques, the lifeguard, warned Heather to stop swimming.

6. Heather from America kept swimming across the pool because she didn't speak French.

7. Finally, Jacques jumped into the water and swam to Heather.

8. Jacques, out of breath, touched Jolene's shoulder, and Jolene jumped in the air.

Page 34 Conjunction Connection

Answers will vary.

Page 37 *Participle Hunt*

Participle	Past or Present?	Modifies
tattered	past	sign
missing	present	cat's
Feeling	present	sad
bent	past	tail
splashing	present	mockingbirds and sparrows
Wondering	present	Babe
mourning	present	dove
lost	past	cat

Stories will vary.

Page 38 *Modifiers on the Loose*

1. Pretending to sweep the street, clowns came by on stilts.
2. A shiny red fire engine carried firefighters burnt by the sun.
3. Bicyclists pedaled in front of the Corn Queen riding on a float.
4. The queen threw popcorn popped that morning to the crowd.
5. Dressed like ears of corn, a group of children marched after the float.
6. At the end of the parade, Suzanne spotted Mayor Hurley riding a camel.

7-9. *Answers will vary.*

Page 41 *What Is This all About?*

1. people
2. Elvis
3. sandwiches
4. Mary Jenkins Langston

Possible Answers:

5. Question: Who always wanted his food prepared quickly?
   Answer: Elvis
6. Question: What were part of Elvis's huge breakfasts?
   Answer: biscuits, eggs, bacon, and sausage
7. Question: Who placed Elvis on a special diet?
   Answer: doctors
8. Question: Who smuggled hot dogs into the hospital?
   Answer: Ms. Langston

Page 42 *We're in Complete Agreement*

1. Williams sisters/have played
2. they/are
3. sisters/hit
4. This/makes

5. Serena/surfs/skateboards
6. biography/reveals; blue/is
7. Venus/is/weighs
8. Neither/enjoys
9-10. *Answers will vary.*

Page 43 *Subjects and Verbs Tragically Separated*

1. The <u>man</u> (wearing the stack of purple hats) (look/looks) silly.
2. <u>Afternoons</u> (on the Great Plains) (gets/get) hot.
3. <u>People</u> (who spend a lot of time outdoors) (protect/protects) themselves.
4. <u>None</u> (of them) (is/are) foolish enough to leave a purple hat at home.
5. In the spring, <u>hundreds</u> (of wildflowers) (dots/dot) the prairie.
6. <u>Butterflies</u> (of every type) (floats/float) across the tall grasses.
7. <u>Children</u> (smearing sunscreen on their noses) (watches/watch) the butterflies.
8. A <u>woman</u> (with two cameras) (snaps/snap) pictures of the children.

Page 45 *Sentence Detective*

1. complete
2. complete
3. run-on; Cheetahs reach speeds of seventy miles per hour, and chickens run nine miles per hour.
4. fragment; Giant tortoises are slow moving animals.
5. fragment; Perhaps because their legs are short, pigs average eleven miles per hour.
6. run-on; Cheetahs are the fastest animals, and garden snails are the slowest.
7. complete
8. complete